Instant Team Foundation Server 2012 and Project Server 2010 Integration How-to

Successfully perform and understand how to integrate your Team Foundation Server 2012 and Project Server 2010

Gary P. Gauvin

PUBLISHING

BIRMINGHAM - MUMBAI

Instant Team Foundation Server 2012 and Project Server 2010 Integration How-to

First published: February 2013

Production Reference: 1190213

Published by Packt Publishing Ltd.
Livery Place
35 Livery Street
Birmingham B3 2PB, UK.

ISBN 978-1-84968-854-3

www.packtpub.com

Credits

Author
Gary P. Gauvin

Reviewer
Mathias Olausson

Acquisition Editor
Grant Mizen

Lead Technical Editor
Meeta Rajani

Technical Editor
Veena Pagare

Copy Editor
Alfida Paiva

Project Coordinator
Esha Thakker

Proofreader
Mario Cecere

Graphics
Aditi Gajjar

Production Coordinator
Conidon Miranda

Cover Work
Conidon Miranda

Cover Image
Aditi Gajjar

About the Author

Gary P. Gauvin has worked in the software development industry for over 20 years, spanning many industries and disciplines. Gary is a Microsoft MVP in the ALM specialty, working closely with Microsoft on the Team Foundation Server 2012 release. He has consulted and worked for the nation's top technology companies. Gary lives and works in Northern NH. You can follow his blog at http://www.theCTO.org. Feel free to connect with him on LinkedIn at www.linkedin.com/in/garypgauvin.

Gary is currently the Application Lifecycle Manager at CD-adapco, the leading provider of the CFD (Computational Fluid Dynamics) software. Gary has held senior positions in many of the nation's top companies as well as in the consultation firm he founded.

I would like to thank my family for putting up with the long hours and short deadlines this project required. I'd also like to thank my co-workers from my former and current employers for putting up with my ranting and raving about this project for months. A big thanks also goes out to the entire MVP community for entertaining my long questions on the mailing lists sometimes, and of course the Visual Studio and Project Server teams that assisted me when needed. Last, but definitely not the least, I'd like to thank the Packt Publishing team (especially Meeta and Esha) for their help with the editing and formatting of this book, without them this project would not even have started.

About the Reviewer

Mathias Olausson works as the ALM Practice Lead for theTranscendent Group, specializing in software craftsmanship and application lifecycle management. With over 15 years of experience as a software consultant and trainer, he has worked in numerous projects and organizations, which have been very valuable when using Visual Studio as a tool for improving the way we build the software. Olausson has been a Microsoft Visual Studio ALM MVP for four years. He is also active as a Visual Studio ALM Ranger, most recently in the role of Project Lead for the Visual Studio Lab Management Guide project. Olausson is a frequent speaker on Visual Studio and Team Foundation Server at conferences and industry events and blogs at `http://msmvps.com/blogs/molausson`.

He has also worked on *Pro Application Lifecycle Management with Visual Studio 2012 (Apress, 1430243449)*.

www.PacktPub.com

Support files, eBooks, discount offers and more

You might want to visit www.PacktPub.com for support files and downloads related to your book.

Did you know that Packt offers eBook versions of every book published, with PDF and ePub files available? You can upgrade to the eBook version at www.PacktPub.com and as a print book customer, you are entitled to a discount on the eBook copy. Get in touch with us at service@packtpub.com for more details.

At www.PacktPub.com, you can also read a collection of free technical articles, sign up for a range of free newsletters and receive exclusive discounts and offers on Packt books and eBooks.

http://PacktLib.PacktPub.com

Do you need instant solutions to your IT questions? PacktLib is Packt's online digital book library. Here, you can access, read and search across Packt's entire library of books.

Why Subscribe?

- Fully searchable across every book published by Packt
- Copy and paste, print and bookmark content
- On demand and accessible via web browser

Free Access for Packt account holders

If you have an account with Packt at www.PacktPub.com, you can use this to access PacktLib today and view nine entirely free books. Simply use your login credentials for immediate access.

Table of Contents

Preface

This book is great for either a beginner of Team Foundation Server or a Project Server administrator with just an idea of how the other product operates and wants to get both the Team Foundation Server and Project Server talking. It is not an exhaustive technical volume of the operation of either TFS or Project Server. Basic step-by-step instructions as well as many helpful tips are given in the book. Readers are expected to know some basic Windows Server commands and account management, and have administrative access to the servers being configured. If you are an experienced Team Foundation Server or Project Server administrator who is upgrading, you'll probably want to just skim the first and last part of the book, and jump into the *Installing Integration* recipe to get just what you need.

What this book covers

Planning for a Successful Integration, helps us examine what's needed to ensure that your integration is successful. It covers the prerequisites and the planning needed to begin, scenarios for various environments, and a few tips to set you up for success.

Installing Integration, looks at installing the Team Foundation Server Extensions for Project Server. We examine the steps and commands involved, a few errors that you may encounter, and how to work around them. We also look at an upgrade scenario and several considerations with it.

Configuration of Initial Permissions, looks at the minimum permissions you will need to configure for a successful installation. Permissions are, by and large, the single area in the integration where people get hung up.

Initial Integration Configuration, provides you the step-by-step instructions to initially configure the integration, including the tools needed and command options available. You'll probably need to continue this for your specific scenario.

Permissions and Security, takes a more detailed look at the permissions you'll need to configure after installation. Additionally, we cover the steps you need to perform to successfully accomplish this. If yours is an enterprise scenario, this is a good starting point but you will still need to do a detailed security assessment with your systems administrator.

Managing Project Server Integration, looks at the basic management steps and verifies that the newly installed system is working correctly. Like the *Permissions and Security* recipe, this is a good starting point, but some detailed planning with your project teams will be needed.

What you need for this book

To begin with, you will need a basic understanding of Windows Server, Team Foundation Server, Visual Studio, and Project Server. This book also expects that the initial installations for these products have already been completed and they are functional.

Who this book is for

This book is great for either a beginner of Team Foundation Server or Project Server administrator with just an idea of how the other product operates and wants to get both the Team Foundation Server and Project Server talking. It is not an exhaustive technical volume of the operation of either TFS or Project Server.

Conventions

In this book, you will find a number of styles of text that distinguish between different kinds of information. Here are some examples of these styles, and an explanation of what they mean.

Code words in text are shown as follows: "This user will be using the command line tool TFSAdmin."

A block of code is set as follows:

```
function Add-SysAdmin
{
    param (
        [System.String] $localSqlInstance = 'SqlExpress',
        [System.String] $loginName = "Builtin\Administrators"
    )
```

Any command-line input or output is written as follows:

```
TfsAdmin ProjectServer /RegisterPWA /pwa:http://tfspsdemo/PWA /
tfs:http://tfspsdemo:8080/tfs/
```

New terms and **important words** are shown in bold. Words that you see on the screen, in menus or dialog boxes for example, appear in the text like this: "In the **Application Management** section, click on **Manage Service Applications**."

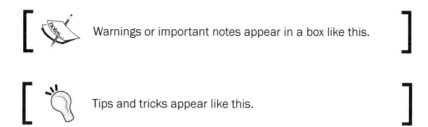

Warnings or important notes appear in a box like this.

Tips and tricks appear like this.

Reader feedback

Feedback from our readers is always welcome. Let us know what you think about this book— what you liked or may have disliked. Reader feedback is important for us to develop titles that you really get the most out of.

To send us general feedback, simply send an e-mail to feedback@packtpub.com, and mention the book title via the subject of your message.

If there is a book that you need and would like to see us publish, please send us a note in the **SUGGEST A TITLE** form on www.packtpub.com or e-mail suggest@packtpub.com.

If there is a topic that you have expertise in and you are interested in either writing or contributing to a book, see our author guide on www.packtpub.com/authors.

Customer support

Now that you are the proud owner of a Packt book, we have a number of things to help you to get the most from your purchase.

Downloading the example code

You can download the example code files for all the Packt books you have purchased from your account at http://www.PacktPub.com. If you purchased this book elsewhere, you can visit http://www.PacktPub.com/support and register to have the files e-mailed directly to you.

Errata

Although we have taken every care to ensure the accuracy of our content, mistakes do occur. If you find a mistake in one of our books—maybe a mistake in the text or the code—we would be grateful if you could report this to us. By doing so, you can save other readers from frustration and help us improve the subsequent versions of this book. If you find any errata, please report them by visiting http://www.packtpub.com/support, selecting your book, clicking on the **errata submission form** link, and entering the details of your errata. Once your errata are verified, your submission will be accepted and the errata will be uploaded on our website, or added to any list of existing errata, under the Errata section of that title. Any existing errata can be viewed by selecting your title from http://www.packtpub.com/support.

Piracy

Piracy of copyright material on the Internet is an ongoing problem across all media. At Packt, we take the protection of our copyright and licenses very seriously. If you come across any illegal copies of our works, in any form, on the Internet, please provide us with the location address or website name immediately so that we can pursue a remedy.

Please contact us at copyright@packtpub.com with a link to the suspected pirated material.

We appreciate your help in protecting our authors, and our ability to bring you valuable content.

Questions

You can contact us at questions@packtpub.com if you are having a problem with any aspect of the book, and we will do our best to address it.

Instant Team Foundation Server 2012 and Project Server 2010 Integration How-to

Welcome to Instant Team Foundation Server 2012 and Project Server 2010 Integration How-to. Here we will cover the initial setup of the powerful integration capabilities that exist between Team Foundation Server and Project Server. It should be noted that the content of the book is based on pre-release software and believed to be accurate at the time of publication.

Planning for a successful integration (Must know)

We will examine what's needed to ensure that your integration is successful. We'll cover the prerequisites and the planning needed to begin, the scenarios for test or production environments, and the different types of synchronization that are possible.

Getting ready

Using Team Foundation Server Extensions for the Project Server, project managers can make the Project Server access real-time project status and resource availability of teams who work in Team Foundation Server. Following the successful configuration of the two server products, the synchronization engine maintains the scheduling of data and resource usage in the mapped Project Server enterprise project plan and Team Foundation Server team project.

How to do it...

There are a few pieces of information we need to collect and a few configuration tasks that we need to make sure have been completed properly.

Here is an installation and configuration requirement checklist to make sure that we are ready to begin:

Installation and configuration requirement checklist

- Sever names for each server involved: Project Server 2010 and Team Foundation Server 2012.
- Service account names and login information: You'll want this information to be handy throughout the tasks in this book. See the *Active Directory – Highly recommended for production installations* section at the end of this chapter.
- Visual Studio 2012 must be installed on the same machine that will be used to configure the integration of the two server products, and on any machine you will use to configure the integration. This does not need to be on one of the server machines.
- Project Server 2010 must be updated to SP1. This product's installation and initial configuration will need to be verified operationally (not covered in this book).
- Project Professional 2010, or Project Professional 2007 SP2 with the KB980209 hotfix (`http://support.microsoft.com/kb/980209`), or Project Professional 2007 with SP3 must be installed on your administration machine.
- The SharePoint web application for the instance of Project Web Access or **PWA** (**Project Web App**) must be set to Classic Mode Authentication. You will not be able to register it if the authentication is set to Claims Based Authentication.
- Visual Studio Team Foundation Server 2012 will need to be installed on each application-tier server that hosts Team Foundation Server and that will participate in synchronizing data with Project Server. This product's installation and initial configuration will need to be verified operationally (not covered in this book).
- Team Foundation Server Extensions for Project Server will be needed later on during the installation. For now, just locate the Team Foundation Server 2012 DVD.

Now that the common pre-configuration items are out of the way, we can move on with the planning.

How it works...

At the core of this integration are the work items in Team Foundation Server, which synchronize with the Tasks in Microsoft Project plans in Project Server. Using this integration, project managers and software development teams can use whichever tools work best for them, and share information transparently.

The integration and all products involved in it are scalable from installations of a few users to several thousands. You can easily scale this integration out by using multiple Project Web Access servers mapped to a multi-server, that is, TFS deployment. We'll cover the specifics of the integration in a later section, but this is a good spot for an overview diagram.

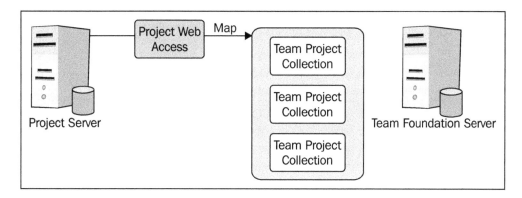

There's more...

We have a few final points to keep in mind, and some valuable tips to make your installations go smoothly. This will not be a complicated integration if we follow the given advice.

A time saver for your test installations

We all know it can take a serious amount of time to build your own testing and demonstration virtual machines. This is especially tough when you are just going to use it for a test installation or a pitch to technical management. Although the following VM link provided by Microsoft is one revision older than the one discussed here, it is much quicker to upgrade this one than to do a fresh installation. For more information, see the following page on the Microsoft website:

`http://go.microsoft.com/fwlink/?LinkID=196413`

You weren't planning a test environment? Now would also be a good time to plan a test system in your deployment schedule. It will not only help you to have an environment to test out configuration changes but will also be a good safety measure to ensure all your mapping is correct before you deploy to a production environment.

Active Directory – Highly recommended for production installations

Active Directory is technically not required; however, it is highly recommended that you deploy Active Directory in your network. It will help with synchronization of the user accounts, groups, and services within Team Foundation Server and Project Server. Otherwise you'll be doing this manually between the two environments. If you haven't deployed Active Directory yet, but are planning to deploy it, now would be a good time to begin that.

SharePoint Authentication mode

We mentioned this in the previous checklist, but it bears repeating here. The authentication that is assigned to the SharePoint web application for the instance of PWA must be set to Classic Mode Authentication. You will not be able to register the instance of PWA if the authentication is set to Claims Based Authentication.

Backup

A server-based product cannot be mentioned completely without a discussion of backup. Do not begin any production installation or upgrade of any product mentioned here without involving a prior backup of all systems. Special attention should be paid to the backup of the Team Foundation Server system. If done improperly, the backup will put your TFS installation into an unusable state after a restore operation, and the worst part will be you won't know this until you start using it again. Please review Microsoft's current recommendation about using marked transactions in your backup strategy with the help of the *Understanding Backing Up Team Foundation Server* document, which is is available at:

`http://msdn.microsoft.com/en-us/library/ms253151.aspx`

Installing integration (Must know)

We'll be installing the Team Foundation Server Extensions for Project Server in this section.

Getting ready

In the previous recipe, we prepared the information that we needed to ensure a successful integration. Now we'll build off that as we install and configure the integration. Please take a moment to review the checklist before we begin. Our first decision point is whether or not this will be a test or production instance. While the installation process is the same in either case, the configuration has some variations to consider.

Prepare Infrastructure	Install / Upgrade Team Foundation Server Extensions	Connect!
Verify Hardware / Software requirements for each product. This my be on the local or remote Project Server. Follow the checklist in the prior section completely to ensure you got all the information you need, perform patched and updates as described	Remove the "old" version if required for an upgrade (don't worry, your data will not be deleted during this unistall of TFS). You may also be upgrading the TFS to 2012. If so, perform that now and verify functionality before continuing.	Carefully follow the sections on setting permissions on all environments. Most problems encountered can be traced back to not setting the required permissions. When this is done we'll walk through the initial mappings and setup required to run the integration

Installation overview

How to do it...

The steps to install Team Foundation Server Extensions for Project Server are fairly simple. The server steps are as follows:

1. Insert the Team Foundation Server 2012 DVD / ISO in the drive, navigate to the `Project Server Extensions` folder, and launch the `tfs_projectServerExtensions.exe` file to begin.

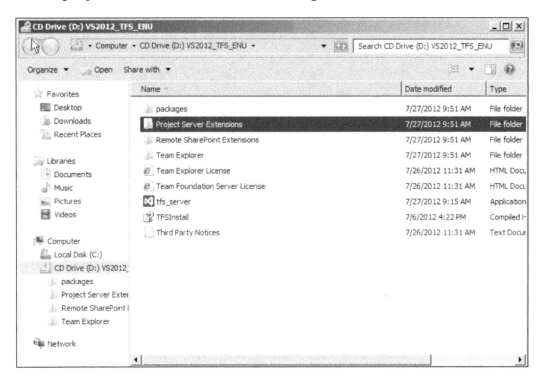

2. In the license terms' dialog box, accept the license terms, and then select **continue**.

3. When the next screen appears, select **Install Now**.

4. On the last screen, select **Close**. You are now done with the installation.

An indication that you didn't remove the old Team Foundation Server 2010 Integration prior to attempting to upgrade to the 2012 edition will appear on the screen. You'll need to remove it with the **Programs and Features** dialog box in the **Control Panel** console to continue, as shown in the following screenshot:

A successful installation will be indicated with the following dialog box:

Success!

Installing the client side is just as simple; following are the steps:

1. Remove Visual Studio 2010 from the client machine.
2. Locate the Visual Studio 2012 installation media and install Visual Studio 2012 on the client machine, following the instructions as prompted.

As discussed in the previous recipe, there are a number of prerequisites and client software that need to be installed. On each machine that will be used by a project manager to synchronize data between enterprise project plans and team projects, you will need to install both Visual Studio 2012 and Microsoft Visual Studio Team Explorer. In reality, the only reason you need Visual Studio is the add-in list. However, as far as this book is concerned, the only way to get the Visual Studio 2012 add-in list is to install a copy of Visual Studio 2012.

There's more...

Although we have covered most of the key parts already, there are a few other things you might want to consider. We'll cover those in the following sections.

Extension versions must match

A common scenario now is upgrading the Team Foundation Server versions to Team Foundation Server 2012. If this is your situation, you should uninstall the extensions from the Project Server and then install the latest version of the Team Foundation Server Extensions for the Project Server on all the servers where it was previously installed. The general order of operations in this case would be:

1. Uninstall Team Foundation Server 2010 and any extensions. Don't worry, all the configuration data is stored in TFS's database, which the upgrade process will detect.
2. Install/upgrade to Team Foundation Sever 2012 as per the installation guide.
3. Install/upgrade the Team Foundation Server Extensions as described in the previous recipe.

64-bit machines now required

Visual Studio Team Foundation Server 2012 now requires a 64-bit machine, as do the Team Foundation Server Extensions for the Project Server.

No remapping needed

Some good news for upgraders; you will not need to unregister any previously mapped components prior to upgrading.

No additional Client Access License (CAL) needed

More good news; although you need to install Visual Studio 2012 to get the add-in list for Microsoft Project Professional, Microsoft tells us that we will not need a CAL to interface with the integration itself.

Note for upgraders from TFS2010

It has been reported that the installation procedure for Team Foundation Server 2012 *may* switch the service account from a specified domain account to a network service. If this occurs, you will need to switch it back to the account you noted in earlier sections while preparing for the installation. Alternatively, you can reset the project server permissions based on this new account. This can be done using the TFS administration console.

Configuration of initial permissions (Must know)

We'll cover the initial permission configuration required and the steps to get you through configuring these for Team Foundation Server Extensions and Project Server in this recipe. These are not all the permissions required for setting up the complete system, but just the ones required to begin configuration. It is possible that in a large enterprise installation, you will need to separate the requests to get them set by several individuals. This should help with facilitating that.

Getting ready

In the previous recipe, we installed the integration. Now we'll build off of that as we configure the integration. Please take a moment to review the work we've done previously before we begin.

Also, it might be handy at this point to review the summary for steps that we will be following in this recipe and in other recipes:

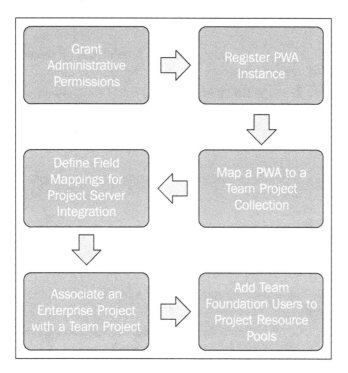

Entire configuration workflow

To initially configure the permissions required, you will need to assign administrative permissions of Team Foundation Server and an instance of **Project Web App** (**PWA**) to a user who will be responsible for the configuration of these products. You will use the **Team Foundation Server Administration Console** page for most of the Team Foundation Server permissions, and the **Project Security** dialog box or **Manage Users / Manage Groups** web pages for PWA. Please note that these are the *minimum* configurations you'll need to perform for permissions; your installation may need more, depending on your specific site requirements.

How to do it...

We'll lay the steps out in the following section by subject to make it easy to follow and refer back to later. Firstly, we will be setting the initial permissions. You should perform the following modifications in the given order:

1. **Adding a user to the Team Foundation Administrators group**:

   Account(s): This is the account(s) that will be used to configure the integration of the Team Foundation Server. If this is the same user who installed Team Foundation Server, then this task would already be done during that product's installation and configuration.

   1. Open the **Team Foundation Server Administration Console** page from the **Start** menu of the Team Foundation Server.

   2. Navigate to the **Group Membership** dialog (**Team Foundation Server Administration Console | Application Tier | Group Membership**) to add this account to the **Team Foundation Administrators** group.

   [This user will be using the command-line tool TFSAdmin; this will be installed by Visual Studio 2012 during its installation.]

2. **Setting the Administer Project Server integration permission to Allow the account**:

   Account(s): These are the accounts of the project managers or other users who will manage the mapping of enterprise projects.

   1. Open the **Team Foundation Server Administration Console** page from the **Start** menu of the Team Foundation Server.

   2. Navigate to the **Team Foundation Server Administration Console | Team Project Collections | Administer Security** dialog box to add the account to set the Administer Project Server permission to allow the user or group.

This is a Project Collection level permission.

3. **Granting the Manage Security global permission to each instance of PWA that you will register with Team Foundation Server**:

Account(s): This is the account(s) of the user who will configure the integration of Team Foundation Server and Project Server or the one who registers the instances of PWA with the Team Foundation Server service account for Team Foundation Server.

1. Open the PWA Site in Internet Explorer at `http://tfspsdemo/PWA/default.aspx`.

2. Navigate to **Project Web App | Edit User | Selected User | Global Permissions Section | Manage Security**.

 Every service account for Project Server and SharePoint Products must be granted interactive logon permissions for the computer on which the service is running. This is not a usual permission for services, so it bears special mentioning. You will need to repeat this on every PWA instance.

4. **Granting Full Control permissions to invoke the Project Server Service Application**:

Account(s): This is the service account for Team Foundation Server.

We will use SharePoint Central Administration using the following steps:

1. Run the **SharePoint Central Administration** page from the **Start** menu.

2. In the **Application Management** section, click on the **Manage Service Applications** option (many service applications will be listed here normally).

3. From the **Manage Service Applications** page, select the row for the Project Server Service Application by clicking within the row but not right on the name of the application; that is, don't double click on it. If you do, no big deal, you just need to go back to the previous step and try it again.

The ribbon should then become available.

1. In the ribbon you should see a **Permissions** icon; click on the **Permissions** icon now.

2. Within the **Connection Permissions for Project Server Service Application dialog** box, enter the name of the service account you will be using for this service, and then click on **Add**. You can go back and change this later if you need to.

3. In the middle pane, ensure that the name of the service account that you just added is still highlighted; if not, please highlight it now.

4. From the bottom pane, select the **Full Control** checkbox then click on **OK**.

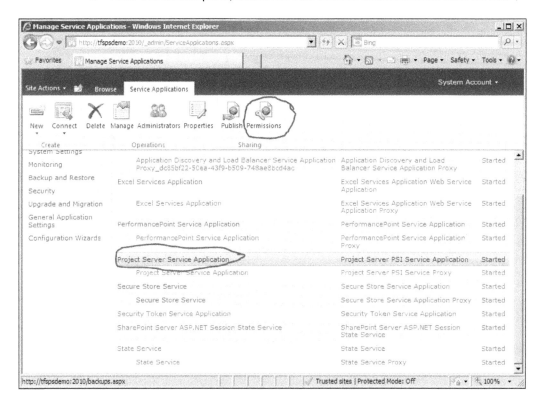

SharePoint central administration, Service Application permissions

5. **Granting SQL Server database permissions**:

Account(s): This is the service account for the web application pool for Project Server 2010 (you can find this by opening **Application Pools** in **IIS Manager | Connections**).

 Since the following commands can take some time, there is also a handy PowerShell script you can use, which is at the end of the *Summary* section.

We will grant permissions to PWA databases of the service account for the web application pool for Project Server 2010.

To enable data synchronization, you need to grant permissions to the service account for the web application pool to update two SQL Server databases for each instance of PWA for Project Server 2010.

To grant permissions to a database for an instance of PWA:

1. Log on to the data-tier server for Project Server.

2. Select **SQL Server Management Studio** from **Start | All Programs | Microsoft SQL Server 2008**.

3. The **Connect to Server** dialog box will now open.

4. In the **Server type** list, select **Database Engine**.

5. In **Server name**, type the name of the server that hosts the databases for Project Server, and then select **Connect**. (If SQL Server is installed on a cluster, type the name of the cluster, not the computer's name. If you have specified a named instance, type the server and instance name in the following format: `DatabaseServer\InstanceName`. If you have Project Server and SQL Server installed on the same machine, the *localhost* name that this dialog box defaults to will work fine.) The **Microsoft SQL Server Management Studio** page opens.

6. Expand the **Databases** option, open the shortcut menu for the database for the instance of PWA (for example, `PWA_Reporting`), and then select **Properties**.

7. Under the **Select a page** list, select **Permissions**.

8. Add the service account of the web application pool for Project Server, and grant the required permissions. For example, the following permissions for the reporting database are required: **Alter any Schema**, **Create Table**, **Delete**, **Execute**, **Insert**, **Select**, and **Update**.

9. On the publishing database (PWA_Published), grant the **Select** permission.

10. Repeat steps 7 through 10 for each instance of PWA that will participate in data synchronization with Team Foundation Server.

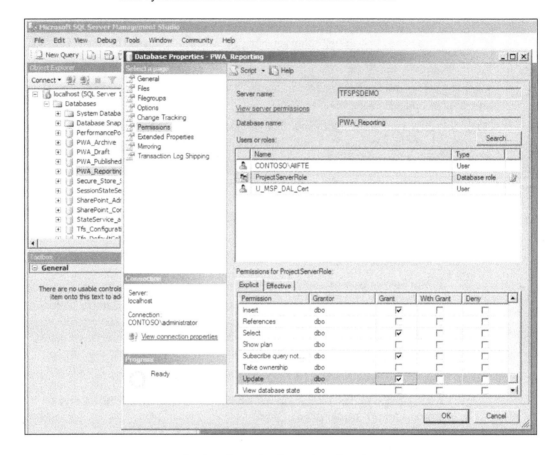

Database Properties, Permissions dialog box

6. **Adding account(s) to the Team Members group of PWA**:

   Account(s): These are the Team Foundation Server team members who will submit the status updates to the Project Server from a client of Team Foundation.

   1. Open the PWA site.

   2. In the PWA SharePoint site, add team members to the **Team Members** group for the PWA, or you must grant them the following minimum set of project permissions, namely **Open Project** and **View Project Site**.

7. **Granting permissions to contribute to the team project in Team Foundation Server**:

   Account(s): These are the users of Project Professional who will publish plans to Team Foundation.

   1. Open the Team Foundation Server Administration Console from the Start Menu.
   2. In Team Foundation Server Administration Console, grant the View Project-level information permissions in Team Foundation, or assign them as members of the Reader group for the team project.

There's more...

Although we've covered most of the key parts already, there are a few other things you might want to consider. We'll cover those in the following section.

If some of the steps given here are not detailed enough for you, do not worry. We cover many of the same ones in the recipe, *Permissions and Security*.

Initial integration configuration (Should know)

These are the minimal steps you'll need to perform in order to complete the initial configuration of Team Foundation Server and Project Server. You may need more steps depending on specific site requirements. Please complete them in the order listed for predictable results.

Getting ready

In order to run the `TfsAdmin` command-line tool indicated in some of these steps, you will need to run it in an elevated command prompt (right-click on the command prompt in the **Start** menu and select **Run as administrator**).

How to do it...

We'll lay the steps out here by subject to make it easy to follow and refer back to later.

Integration

You'll also need to change the directory to `C:\Program Files (x86)\Microsoft Visual Studio 11.0\Common7\IDE`, or add it to your path. Open the **Command Prompt** console from the **Start** menu. Using the following steps you can perform integration:

1. Register an instance of PWA. Each instance must be registered.

   Tool used: `TfsAdmin`

   1. Open the **Command Prompt** console from the **Start** menu.
   2. Run the following command:

      ```
      TfsAdmin ProjectServer /RegisterPWA /pwa:<pwaUrl> /
      tfs:<tfsUrl>
      ```

      Replace the `<>` brackets with the URL, as shown in the following code:

      ```
      TfsAdmin ProjectServer /RegisterPWA /pwa:http://tfspsdemo/
      PWA /tfs:http://tfspsdemo:8080/tfs/
      ```

2. Map the PWA instance with a team project collection.

   Tool used: `TfsAdmin`

   1. Open the command prompt from the **Start** menu.
   2. Run the following command (without the <> brackets):

      ```
      TfsAdmin ProjectServer /MapPWAtoCollection /pwa:<pwaUrl> /
      collection:<tpcUrl>
      ```

      Replace the `<>` brackets with the URL, as shown in the following code:

      ```
      TfsAdmin ProjectServer /MapPWAToCollection /pwa:http://
      tfspsdemo/PWA /collection:http://tfspsdemo:8080/tfs/
      DefaultCollection
      ```

    Map each instance of PWA that supports an enterprise project plan.

3. Upload default field mappings.

   Tool used: `TfsAdmin`

   1. Open the command prompt from the **Start** menu.
   2. Run the following command (without the <> brackets):

      ```
      TfsAdmin ProjectServer /UploadFieldMappings /
      collection:<tpcUrl> /useDefaultFieldMappings
      ```

Replace the <> brackets with the URL, as shown in the following code:

```
TfsAdmin ProjectServer /UploadFieldMappings /
collection:http://tfspsdemo:8080/tfs/DefaultCollection /
useDefaultFieldMappings
```

 We must define the field mappings for each project collection that we have mapped to an instance of PWA. You can use the default field mappings to begin with and customize if you need to (many organizations use this right out of the box).

4. Associate an enterprise project plan with a team project.

Tool used: `TfsAdmin`

1. Open **Command Prompt** from the **Start** menu.

2. Run the following command (without the <> brackets):

```
TfsAdmin ProjectServer /MapPlanToTeamProject /
collection:tpcUrl /enterpriseproject:<ProjectServerPlanName>
/teamproject:<TfsProjectName> /workitemtypes:<ListOfTypes>
```

Replace the <> brackets with the URL, as shown in the following code:

```
TfsAdmin ProjectServer /MapPlanToTeamProject /
collection:http://tfspsdemo:8080/tfs/
DefaultCollection/ enterpriseproject:MyEnterpriseProje
ct /teamproject:MyTfsTeamProject /workitemtypes:"User
Story,Task"
```

 Do not include a space after the comma for the `workitemtypes` parameter. If you mapped a plan while it was open, re-open it to register the changes. Look for the **Publish to Team Project** and **Work Item Type** columns to indicate that the mapping has been completed.

The `/nofixedwork` flag is optional. Use this only if you want the Project Server tasks that are mapped to the work items in Team Foundation Server to not be assigned to the Fixed Work task type.

5. Add team members to the enterprise resource pool.

    Tool used: `Project Web App`

    On each task that is published to the team project, you need to assign a valid member of the team project as a resource. You also need to identify any team member who submits work items that are synchronized with Project Server. To identify valid contributors, you must add team members from the enterprise resource pool to the resources for the enterprise project plan.

     Please refer to the detailed instructions at the location *Add Team Foundation members to the Team Members group* in the recipe *Managing Project Server*. Also, please refer to details on this function at `http://office.microsoft.com/en-us/project-help/add-resources-to-the-enterprise-resource-pool-HA010377760.aspx`.

6. Verify the synchronization.

    The last step in setting up the initial integration is to verify the synchronization. Please refer to *Verifying Synchronization* in the recipe *Managing Project Server*.

Permissions and security (Must know)

In this chapter we'll examine the various permissions, service accounts needed, and various roles involved in this integration. We'll also cover the steps you'll need to perform to set each of these. Please keep in mind that depending on your unique environment, and reuse of existing accounts and groups, some of these permissions may have already been granted.

Getting ready

To begin with, we need to make sure we are set up for success. Let's look at this from a server-by-server view:

> ▶ **Team Foundation Server**: In order to perform any of the operations in this chapter, you will need to belong to the **Team Foundation Administrators** group (alternately, you could also assign the view instance-level information and edit instance-level information to allow). You'll also need to have access to the **Team Foundation Server Administration Console** page (alternately, you could also use the **Group Membership** dialog box in **Team Explorer**, but the **Team Foundation Administration Console** page is much easier to work with for this), as shown in the following screenshot:

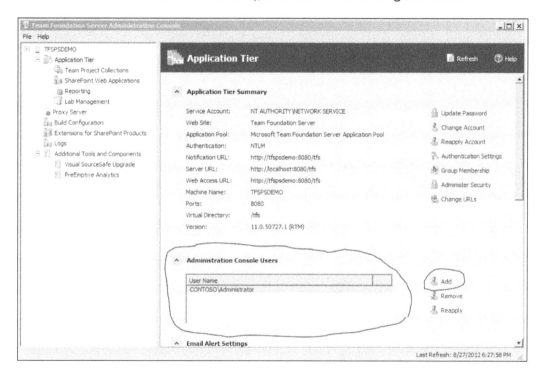

Team Foundation Sever Administration Console

▶ **Project Server**: In Project Server, you'll need the **Manage users and groups** global permission for an instance of Project Web Access or PWA. To set these, you'll need access to the Project Server through PWA.

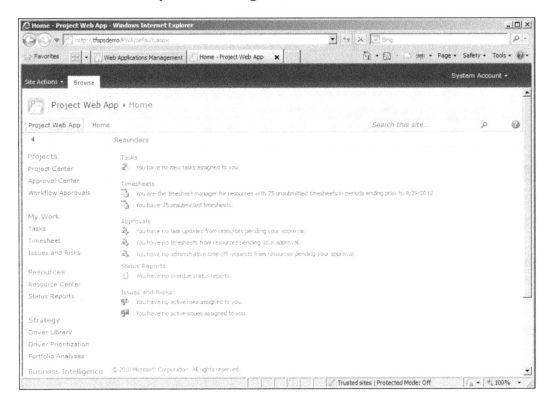

Project Web App

▶ **SQL Server**: To grant Project Server 2010 permissions for the reporting database, you need to be a member of the Administrators Security group for the SQL Server databases for Project Server.

▶ **SharePoint**: In SharePoint, you must belong to the **Farm Administrators** group, the administrators group for the web application that supports Project Server, or the **SharePoint Administration** group. The exact group membership that you will use will depend on the specifics of your deployment.

Required permissions matrix for integration with Project Server 2010 and detailed instructions on how to set these are explained in the following reference table:

Team Foundation Permissions to be set:

Need to Set For:	Team Foundation permissions
Accounts of users who configure the integration by running the `TfsAdmin` and `ProjectServer` commands but who do not register or unregister instances of PWA.	Grant the Administer Project Server integration permission to these users.

Accounts that will need both Team Foundation and Project Server permissions set:

Need to Set For:	Team Foundation permissions	Project Server 2010 permissions
Users who configure the integration by running the `TfsAdmin`, `ProjectServer`, and `RegisterPWA/UnRegisterPWA` commands.	Add these users to the Team Foundation Administrators group.	Add these users to the Administrators group for each instance of PWA that you will register with TFS.
Accounts of users who configure the integration by running `TfsAdmin` and `ProjectServer` commands but who do not register or unregister instances of PWA.	Grant the Administer Project Server integration permission to these users.	N/A.
User accounts assigned as resources in the project plan or to the "Assigned To field for a work" item.	Add the accounts of team members to the contributor group for the team project.	Add team members to the Team Members group for PWA or grant them the Open Project and View Project Site permissions in project. You must also add these accounts to the enterprise project pool and to the resource pool for the project plan.
Accounts of users of Project Professional.	Grant view project-level information or assign them as members of the project Reader group.	Add these accounts to the Project Manager group on Project Server.

Accounts that will need just Project Server permissions:

Need to Set For:	Project Server 2010 permissions
The service account for Team Foundation Server.	Set the following Global and Category permissions to the service account for Team Foundation Server: The Global permissions for the following users are: ▸ Admin: Manage Enterprise Custom Fields, Manage Server Events, Manage Site Services, and Manage Users and Groups ▸ General: Log On, New Task Assignment, and Reassign Task ▸ Project: Build Team on New Project ▸ Views: View Approvals, View Project Center, View Resource Center, and View Task Center The Category permissions for the following users are: ▸ Project: Open Project and View Project Site ▸ Resource: View Enterprise Resource Data Grant Full Control permissions to start the Project Server Service Application.
The service account for the Project Server web application pool.	Grant the service account for the Project Server web application pool. The following are the SQL Server permissions for the PWA reporting database: ▸ Alter any Schema ▸ Create Table ▸ Delete ▸ Execute ▸ Insert ▸ Select ▸ Update For the `PWA Publish` database, grant the Select permission.
The Service account for the Project Server event handler.	Full Control permissions to the Project Server Service Application.

How to do it...

We'll lay the steps out here by subject to make it easy to follow and refer back to later.

- ▸ **Granting Team Foundation Administrative permissions**:

    In order to configure the integration of Team Foundation Server and Project Server, you must have permissions to administer Team Foundation Server or at least a team project collection. For both configuration and synchronization, you must also grant permission to administer Project Server integration to the user who will configure the integration of the two server products. Following are the steps to show how to grant these permissions:

    1. Launch the **Team Foundation Server Administration Console** page.

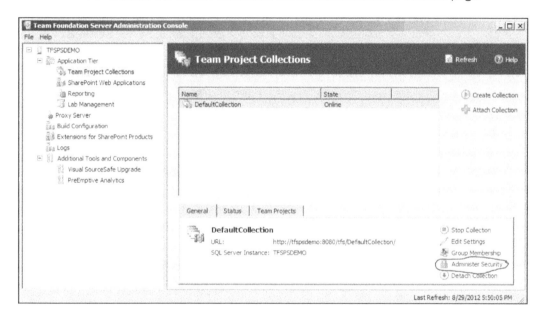

Team Foundation Server Administration Console, Administer Security

    Expand the server node (**Application Tier**), click on **Team Project Collections**, click on a collection, and then click on the **Administer Security** option.

    2. In the **Global Security** window, click on **[Collection]\Project Collection Service Accounts**.

    3. Under the **Permissions** section for the Administer Project Server integration, select the **Allow** checkbox.

    4. Click on the **Close** option to close the **Global Security** window.

▶ **Granting Project Server permissions**:

You need to grant the following minimal Project Server permissions:

1. Add the account of the user who will register an instance of PWA to Team Foundation Server to the administrators group.

2. Either add the service account for Team Foundation Server to the administrators group, or grant that account the minimum set of Global and Category permissions as described in the previous reference table.

3. Add the accounts of any Team Foundation members who will submit status updates to Project Server to the Team Members group.

▶ **Adding an account to Project Server and assigning it to the administrators group for Project Server 2010**:

1. From the PWA home page, in the **Quick Launch** area (from the side menu, on the left-hand side, scroll all the way down) select **Server Settings**.

2. From the **Server Settings** page, select **Manage Users**.

3. From the **Manage Users** page, select **New User**. This will begin the creation of a new user account. You will return here as needed for adding additional administrators.

4. On the **New User** page, enter at least the required fields. Some things to keep in mind as you are doing this are:

   ❏ Uncheck the checkbox for **User can be assigned as a resource** if the account is a service account. This would be left as default for normal users, but not for an administrator.

   ❏ In the **User Authentication** field, enter the account name of the user or the service account you want to use.

   ❏ Uncheck the checkbox for **Resource can be leveled** if the account is an administrator or a service account. This would be left as default for normal users, but not for an administrator as noted previously.

   ❏ Lastly, you'll need to add the account to the Administrators group; from **Security Groups**, select **Administrators** in the list and then click on **Add**.

5. Click on **Save**.

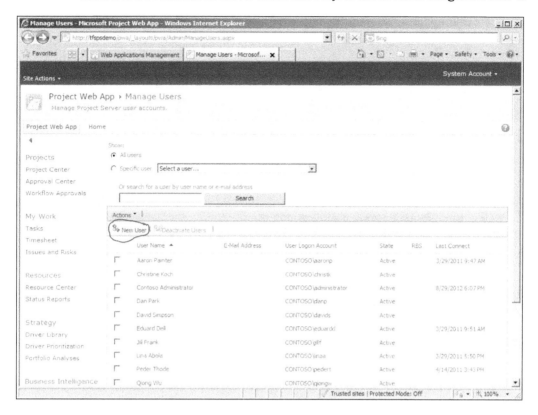

Project Web App, New User

▶ **Granting the minimum Global permissions to the service account for Team Foundation Server:**

1. From the **PWA** page, in the **Quick Launch** area click on the **Server Settings** option.

2. From the **Server Settings** page, click on **Manage Users**.

3. From the **Manage Users** page, click on **New User**.

4. From the **New User** page, type the required information in each field. Note the following:

   ❑ Clear the checkbox for **User can be assigned as a resource** because the account is a service account.

   ❑ For user authentication, type the account name of the service account.

   ❑ To assign Global permissions, select the **Allow** checkbox for each permission that you want to set, as specified earlier in this topic.

5. Click on **Save**.

▸ **Granting Category permissions to the service account**:

1. From the home page for PWA, in the **Quick Launch** area click on the **Server Settings** option.

2. From the **Server Settings** page, click on the **Manage Categories** option.

3. From the **Manage Categories** page, click on the **New Category** option.

4. From the **Add or Edit Category** page, type a name for the service account category. For example, type `Servicing Account`.

5. Under the **Available Users** list, click on the name of the service account for Team Foundation Server, and then click on **Add**.

6. Under the **Projects** list, click on the **All current and future projects in Project Server database** option.

7. Click on **Save**.

▸ **Adding Team Foundation members to the Team Members group**:

1. From the home page for PWA, in the **Quick Launch** area click on the **Server Settings** option.

2. From the **Server Settings** page, in the **Security** section click on the **Manage Groups** options.

3. From the **Manage Groups** page, click on the **Team Members** option.

4. From the **Add or Edit Group** page, hold down the *Shift* key, click on the users whom you want to add from the **Available Users** list, and then click on **Add**.

5. Under **Categories**, verify or add **My Tasks** from **Available Categories** to **Selected Categories**.

▸ **Adding the Service Account for Team Foundation Server to the Project Server Service Application for Project Server 2010**:

In order to enable status update processing by the synchronization engine for integration with Project Server 2010, you must add the service account for Team Foundation Server to the Project Server Service Application. Alternatively, you could use Windows PowerShell (not covered here).

Following are the steps to add the Service Account using SharePoint Central Administration:

1. Launch the **SharePoint Central Administration** page for Project Server.

2. Under **Application Management**, choose the **Manage service applications** option.

3. From the **Manage Service Applications** page, highlight the **Project Server Service Application** row by clicking within the row but not on the name of the application. The ribbon will now be available.

4. In the ribbon, select the **Permissions** option.

5. In the **Connection Permissions for Project Server Service Application** dialog box, type the name of the service account and then select **Add**.

6. In the middle pane, make sure that the name of the newly added service account is highlighted.

7. In the bottom pane, select the **Full Control** checkbox and then select **OK**.

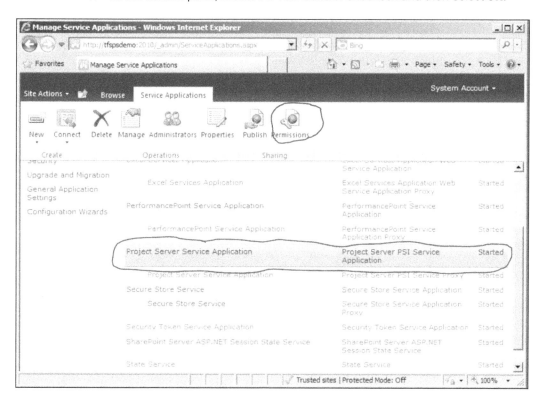

Manage Service Applications dialog box for step 3

▶ **Granting permissions to PWA databases of the service account for the web application pool for Project Server 2010:**

To enable data synchronization, you need to grant permissions to the service account for the web application pool to update two SQL Server databases for each instance of PWA for Project Server 2010.

Following are the steps to grant permissions to a database for an instance of PWA:

1. Log on to the data-tier server for Project Server.

2. Select **SQL Server Management Studio** in **Start | All Programs | Microsoft SQL Server 2008**.

3. The **Connect to Server** dialog box will now open.

4. In the **Server type** list, select **Database Engine**.

5. In the **Server name** field, type the name of the server that hosts the databases for Project Server, and then select **Connect**. (If SQL Server is installed on a cluster, type the name of the cluster, not the computer name. If you have specified a named instance, type the server and instance name in the following format: `DatabaseServer\InstanceName`. If you have Project Server and SQL Server installed on the same machine, the *localhost* name that this dialog box defaults to will work fine.)

6. The **SQL Server Management Studio** page opens.

7. Expand the **Databases** option, open the shortcut menu of the database for the instance of PWA (for example, `PWA_Reporting`), and then select **Properties**.

8. Under **Select a page**, select **Permissions**.

9. Add the service account of the web application pool for Project Server and grant the required permissions. For example, **Alter any Schema**, **Create Table**, **Delete**, **Execute**, **Insert**, **Select**, and **Update** are the permissions required for the reporting database.

10. On the Publishing database (`PWA_Published`), grant the **Select** permission.

11. Repeat steps 7 through 10 for each instance of PWA that will participate in data synchronization with Team Foundation Server.

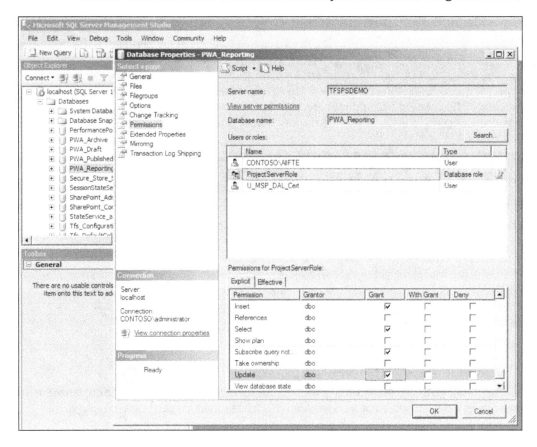

Database Properties, Permissions dialog box for step 8

There's more...

Although we've covered most of the key parts already, there are a few other things you might want to consider. We'll cover those in the following section.

Logon permission for services

You must grant the permission to log on to the computer on which the service is running, to all service accounts for Project Server and SharePoint products.

Service account permissions

The service account for Team Foundation Server also runs the **Team Foundation Background Job Agent Service**. All TfsAdmin commands are run in this service account's context, except for the /**RegisterPWA** and /**UnregisterPWA** options, which are run under the executing user. The Team Foundation Background Job Agent Service manages data synchronization processes. This service account requires permissions to access each instance of PWA that has been mapped, and permissions to call Project Server integration services.

Managing Project Server integration (Should know)

The recipe will detail the commands used to manage the Project Server integration using the TFSAdmin Project Server's command-line tool. Various topics will include verifying synchronization, common command parameters, team project association management, managing the association of enterprise project plans to team projects, work item types, and how to support custom field mapping. There is no particular order of these commands in this section once you pass the verifying synchronization stage. Please use it as a reference when needed.

Getting ready

To begin with, you'll want to start up PWA and the **Team Foundation Server Administration** console. By now you should be very familiar with these tools that you've been using in the previous sections.

How to do it...

We'll lay the steps out here by subject to make it easy to follow and refer back to later.

> ► **Verifying synchronization**:
>
>   First let's complete the work we performed in the recipe *Initial Integration Configuration* by verifying if the synchronization between Project Server and Team Foundation Server is working. At the simplest level, if your tasks are synchronizing properly between the enterprise project in Project Server and the team project in Team Foundation Server, then we can assume that the synchronization (at least some of it) is working.

At a deeper level, we can check the synchronization messages on the server. To perform this, we can use the `TFSAdmin` command-line tool that we should be familiar with by now. Also, in order to run the `TfsAdmin` command-line tool indicated in these steps, you will need to run it in an elevated command prompt (right-click on the **Command Prompt** console in the **Start** menu and select **Run as administrator**). You'll also need to change the directory to `C:\Program Files (x86)\ Microsoft Visual Studio 11.0\Common7\IDE`, or add it to your path. Display the most recent errors that were logged for a team project collection by using the **/ GetSyncMessages** option of the `TFSAdmin ProjectServer` command-line tool. The syntax of the command is as follows:

```
TfsAdmin ProjectServer /GetSyncMessages /collection:tpcUrl
```

As an example, in our demo system we would use:

```
TfsAdmin ProjectServer /GetSyncMessages /collection:http://
tfspsdemo:8080/tfs/DefaultCollection
```

If errors are indicated, you will need to follow up and resolve them on a case-by-case basis. Not all errors indicate a failure to synchronize and may be informational. The ultimate test is whether or not mapped work items are actually being synchronized between the two systems.

▶ **Managing team project association**:

Management of the association of the team project and enterprise project is done with the `TfsAdmin ProjectServer` command-line tool that we've been using throughout the recipes. To synchronize the data between an enterprise project plan and a team project, a project plan must be mapped to a team project. Multiple enterprise project plans can also be mapped to the same TFS team project. Before trying this, please be sure that you have registered and mapped the instance of PWA that is associated with the enterprise project to a team project collection as covered in prior sections. After this is complete, we can map and unmap plans to team projects as required (as we did in a previous recipe). To begin with, let's open a command prompt and change the directory to `C:\Program Files (x86)\ Microsoft Visual Studio 11.0\Common7\IDE`. From here, we are going to use the URLs and PWAs and team project names that are part of our demo server for clarity's sake.

TFS URL: `http://tfspsdemo:8080/tfs`

Collection URL: `http://tfspsdemo:8080/tfs/DefaultCollection`

Also, replace `tpcUrl` with the URL of the team project collection, `EnterpriseProjectName` with the name of the enterprise project plan, and `TeamProjectName` with the name of the team project.

▶ **Listing PWA instances that are registered**:

First let's list the instances of PWA that are already registered. This will give us an idea where to start if this is an existing installation:

1. Open **Command Prompt** from the **Start** menu.

2. In the command prompt you've opened, type the following:

   ```
   TfsAdmin ProjectServer /GetRegisteredPWA /tfs:http://
   tfspsdemo:8080/tfs
   ```

Your results should be similar to the following:

GetRegisteredPWA output

▶ **Listing the project collections that are mapped to a PWA instance**:

Next we'll want to see what collections have been mapped for data synchronization. Keep in mind that you can associate an enterprise project plan only with a team project (in TFS) that is on a collection that has already been mapped to an instance of PWA that contains that particular enterprise project plan.

Following are the steps to list the project collections:

1. Open **Command Prompt** from the **Start** menu.

2. In the command prompt you've opened, type:

   ```
   TfsAdmin ProjectServer /GetMappedCollections /
   tfs:http://tfspsdemo:8080/tfs
   ```

Your results should be similar to the following screenshot:

GetMappedCollections output

▶ **Associating a Project Sever enterprise project plan with a Team Foundation Server team project**:

In order to synchronize a team project with an enterprise project plan, we'll need to associate them by mapping them. We'll be using the `TfsAdmin ProjectServer` command-line tool again. We've already used this command in the previous sections, so it may look familiar.

The following diagram shows the mapping an Enterprise Project to a Team Project workflow:

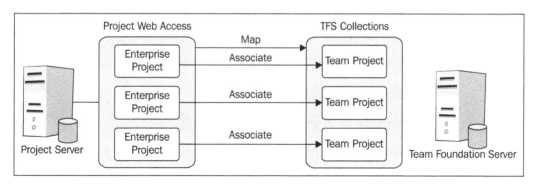

Mapping an Enterprise Project to a Team Project workflow

Following are the steps to map them:

1. Open **Command Prompt** from the **Start** menu.

2. In the command prompt you've opened, type:

```
TfsAdmin ProjectServer /MapPlanToTeamProject /
collection:tpcUrl /enterpriseProject:EnterpriseProjectNa
me /teamProject:TeamProjectName /workItemTypes:ListOfWor
kItemTypes /nofixedwork /projectFieldForWorkItemType:Pro
jectFieldName
```

▶ **Deleting the association between an enterprise project plan and a team project**:

Occasionally, you may want to remove the association you've set up. Before you can do this, you'll need to delete any tasks that are linked to work items in the mapped team project. Although the **/Force** option can override this, it is not recommended unless you are sure that there are no work items currently mapped.

Following are the steps for unmapping:

1. Open **Command Prompt** from the **Start** menu.

2. In the command prompt you've opened, type:

```
TfsAdmin ProjectServer /UnmapPlanFromTeamProject/
collection:tpcUrl /enterpriseProject:EnterpriseProjectNa
me /teamProject:TeamProjectName
```

If successful, you should get an output message similar to the following:

Unmapping enterprise project EnterpriseProjectName from team project TeamProjectName.

Enterprise project EnterpriseProjectName was successfully unmapped from team project TeamProjectName.

Sources of Additional Information

In this section, we'll provide good sources of additional information for further learning and a few more parting reminder tips and where to look for more information.

Service account change during upgrade

It has been reported that the installation procedure for Team Foundation Server 2012 *may* switch the service account from a specified domain account to a network service. If this occurs, you will need to switch it back to the account you noted in earlier recipes while preparing for the installation. Alternatively, you could reset the project server permissions based on this new account. This can be done using the TFS administration console.

A handy SQL permissions script

To make the initial security setup less of a chore (provided you have PowerShell installed on your servers), the following script will help. It grants all local administrators SQL admin permissions. Many thanks to the Visual Studio ALM team that provided the following script:

```
function Add-SysAdmin
{
    param (
        [System.String] $localSqlInstance = 'SqlExpress',
        [System.String] $loginName = "Builtin\Administrators"
    )
    try
    {
    Write-Host ( "Sql Instance: {0}" -f $localSqlInstance )
    Write-Host ( "Login name   : {0}" -f $loginName )
        if ($localSqlInstance -eq '.' -or $localSqlInstance -eq
'MSSQLSERVER')
        {
          # Default instance
          $localSqlInstance = 'MSSQLSERVER'
          $serviceName = 'MSSQLSERVER'
          $dataSource = '.'
        }
        else
        {
          $serviceName = 'MSSQL$' + $localSqlInstance
          $dataSource = 'localhost\' + $localSqlInstance
        }
        $sqlServerService = Get-Service | where {$_.Name -eq $serviceName
    }
```

```
    if ($sqlServerService -eq $null)
    {
        Write-Error ("Cannot find a service with the name: '{0}'.
Verify that you specified correct local SQL Server instance." -f
$serviceName)
        return
    }
    # Stop the service if it is running
    if ($sqlServerService.Status.ToString() -ne "Stopped")
    {
        Write-Host 'Stopping SQL Server'
        $sqlServerService.Stop()
        $sqlServerService.WaitForStatus("Stopped")
    }
    Write-Host 'Starting SQL Server in the admin mode'
    # Start service in admin mode
    $sqlServerService.Start(@("-s", $serviceName, "-m", "-T", "7806"))
    $sqlServerService.WaitForStatus("Running")
    $connectionStringBuilder = New-Object -TypeName System.Data.
SqlClient.SqlConnectionStringBuilder
    $connectionStringBuilder.psbase.DataSource = $dataSource
    $connectionStringBuilder.psbase.IntegratedSecurity = $true
    $sqlConnection = New-Object -TypeName System.Data.SqlClient.
SqlConnection $connectionStringBuilder.psbase.ConnectionString
    Start-Sleep -Seconds 5
    Write-Host 'Connecting to the SQL Server'
    $sqlConnection.Open()
    Write-Host 'Connected to the SQL Server'
    Write-Host ('Adding {0} to the sysadmin server role' -f
$loginName)
    $sqlCommand = $sqlConnection.CreateCommand()
    $sqlCommand.CommandText = "sp_addsrvrolemember"
    $sqlCommand.CommandType = "StoredProcedure"
    $loginParam = $sqlCommand.Parameters.Add("@loginame", $loginName)
    $roleParam = $sqlCommand.Parameters.Add("@rolename", 'sysadmin')
    $temp = $sqlCommand.ExecuteNonQuery()
    Write-Host ('{0} has been added to the sysadmin server role
successfully' -f $loginName)
    # Stop the service if it is running
    Write-Host 'Stopping SQL Server'
    $sqlServerService.Stop()
    $sqlServerService.WaitForStatus("Stopped")
    Write-Host 'Starting SQL Server in the non-admin mode'
    $sqlServerService.Start()
```

```
$sqlServerService.WaitForStatus("Running")
}
catch
{
Write-Error $_
}
}
```

Where to look for more information

Following are a number of good sources of information you can check for items that are not covered here or if you need to go further in depth on them:

▸ You can upgrade a test VM. You can download the Microsoft Hyper-V VM from the following link to practice your own upgrade scenarios:

`http://go.microsoft.com/fwlink/?LinkID=196413`

▸ Check the following Microsoft Technet site for Project Server 2010 for in-depth technical information on the product:

`http://technet.microsoft.com/en-us/library/`
`cc303399(v=office.14).aspx`

▸ Check the following Microsoft site for Visual Studio 2012 for in-depth information on the product:

`http://msdn.microsoft.com/en-us/library/vstudio/dd831853.aspx`

▸ More technical information for the integration itself can be found on *Enable Data Flow Between Team Foundation Server and Microsoft Project Server* page on the following Microsoft MSDN site:

`http://msdn.microsoft.com/en-us/library/gg455680(v=vs.110).aspx`

▸ The Visual Studio team blog site can be found on:

`http://blogs.msdn.com/b/visualstudioalm/`

▸ The author's blog site, which is not specific to Visual Studio or Project Server, but has some interesting ramblings on technical management and Team Foundation Server and where you can also ask questions, can be found on:

`http://www.thecto.org/`

 **Thank you for buying**
Instant Team Foundation Server 2012 and Project Server 2010 Integration How-To

About Packt Publishing

Packt, pronounced 'packed', published its first book "*Mastering phpMyAdmin for Effective MySQL Management*" in April 2004 and subsequently continued to specialize in publishing highly focused books on specific technologies and solutions.

Our books and publications share the experiences of your fellow IT professionals in adapting and customizing today's systems, applications, and frameworks. Our solution based books give you the knowledge and power to customize the software and technologies you're using to get the job done. Packt books are more specific and less general than the IT books you have seen in the past. Our unique business model allows us to bring you more focused information, giving you more of what you need to know, and less of what you don't.

Packt is a modern, yet unique publishing company, which focuses on producing quality, cutting-edge books for communities of developers, administrators, and newbies alike. For more information, please visit our website: www.packtpub.com.

Writing for Packt

We welcome all inquiries from people who are interested in authoring. Book proposals should be sent to author@packtpub.com. If your book idea is still at an early stage and you would like to discuss it first before writing a formal book proposal, contact us; one of our commissioning editors will get in touch with you.

We're not just looking for published authors; if you have strong technical skills but no writing experience, our experienced editors can help you develop a writing career, or simply get some additional reward for your expertise.

**Team Foundation
Server 2012 Starter**

Your quick start guide to TFS 2012, top features, and best practices with hands on examples

Jakob Ehn   Terje Sandstrøm   [PACKT]

Team Foundation Server 2012 Starter [Instant]

ISBN: 978-1-849688-38-3   Paperback: 72 pages

Your quick start guide to TFS 2012, top features, and best practices with hands on examples

1. Learn something new in an Instant! A short, fast, focused guide delivering immediate results.

2. Install TFS 2012 from scratch

3. Get up and running with your first project

4. Streamline release cycles for maximum productivity

**Mastering phpMyAdmin 3.4 for
Effective MySQL Management**

A complete guide to getting started with phpMyAdmin 3.4 and mastering its features

Marc Delisle   PACKT open source

Mastering phpMyAdmin 3.4 for Effective MySQL Management

ISBN: 978-1-849517-78-2   Paperback: 394 pages

A complete guide to getting started with phpMyAdmin 3.4 and mastering its features

1. A step-by-step tutorial for manipulating data with the latest version of phpmyadmin

2. Administer your MySQL databases with phpMyAdmin

3. Manage users and privileges with MySQL Server Administration tools

4. Learn to do things with your MySQL database and phpMyAdmin that you didn't know were possible!

Please check **www.PacktPub.com** for information on our titles

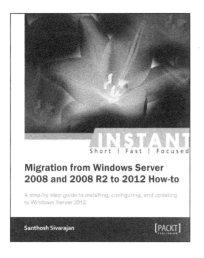

Migration from Windows Server
2008 and 2008 R2 to 2012 How-to

A step-by-step guide to installing, configuring, and updating
to Windows Server 2012

Santhosh Sivarajan

Instant Migration from Windows Server 2008 and 2008 R2 to 2012 How-to [Instant]

ISBN: 978-1-849687-44-7   Paperback: 84 pages

A step-by-step guide to installing, configuring, and
updating to Windows Server 2012

1. Learn something new in an Instant! A short, fast,
   focused guide delivering immediate results.

2. Decommission old servers and convert your
   environment into the Windows Server 2012 native
   environment

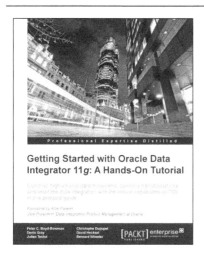

Getting Started with Oracle Data
Integrator 11g: A Hands-On Tutorial

Getting Started with Oracle Data Integrator 11g: A Hands-On Tutorial

ISBN: 978-1-849680-68-4   Paperback: 384 pages

Combine high volume data movement, complex
transformations and real-time data intergration with the
robust capabilities of ODI in this practical guide

1. Discover the comprehensive and sophisticated
   orchestration of data integration tasks made
   possible with ODI, including monitoring and error-
   management

2. Get to grips with the product architecture
   and building data integration processes with
   technologies including Oracle, Microsoft SQL
   Server and XML files

Please check **www.PacktPub.com** for information on our titles